A Note From Rick Renner

I am on a personal quest to see a "revival of the Bible" so people can establish their lives on a firm foundation that will stand strong and endure the test as end-time storm winds begin to intensify.

In order to experience a revival of the Bible in your personal life, it is important to take time each day to read, receive, and apply its truths to your life. James tells us that if we will continue in the perfect law of liberty — refusing to be forgetful hearers, but determined to be doers — we will be blessed in our ways. As you watch or listen to the programs in this series and work through this corresponding study guide, I trust you will search the Scriptures and allow the Holy Spirit to help you hear something new from God's Word that applies specifically to your life. I encourage you to be a doer of the Word He reveals to you. Whatever the cost, I assure you — it will be worth it.

> Thy words were found, and I did eat them;
> and thy word was unto me the joy and rejoicing of mine heart:
> for I am called by thy name, O Lord God of hosts.
> — Jeremiah 15:16

Your brother and friend in Jesus Christ,

Rick Renner

Unless otherwise indicated, all scripture quotations are taken from the *King James Version* of the Bible.

Scripture quotations marked (*AMPC*) are taken from the *Amplified® Bible*. Copyright © 1954, 1958, 1962, 1964, 1965, 1987 by The Lockman Foundation. Used by permission. **www.Lockman.org**.

Scripture quotations marked (*NKJV*) are taken from the *New King James Version®*. Copyright © 1982 by Thomas Nelson. Used by permission. All rights reserved.

Scripture quotations marked (*NLT*) are taken from the Holy Bible, *New Living Translation*, copyright © 1996, 2004, 2015 by Tyndale House Foundation. Used by permission of Tyndale House Publishers, Inc., Carol Stream, Illinois 60188. All rights reserved.

Scripture quotations marked (*MSG*) are taken from *The Message*, copyright © 1993, 2002, 2018 by Eugene H. Peterson. Used by permission of NavPress. All rights reserved. Represented by Tyndale House Publishers, Inc.

Scripture quotations marked *RIV* are taken from *Renner Interpretive Version*. Copyright © 2021 by Rick Renner.

The Fire of God In Your Life
The Benefits of Embracing God's Fiery Presence

Copyright © 2023 by Rick Renner
1814 W. Tacoma St.
Broken Arrow, OK 74012-1406

Published by Rick Renner Ministries
www.renner.org

ISBN 13: 978-1-6675-0314-1

eBook ISBN 13: 978-1-6675-0315-8

All rights reserved. No portion of this book may be reproduced or transmitted in any form or by any means — electronic, mechanical, photocopy, recording, scanning, or other — except for brief quotations in critical reviews or articles, without the prior written permission of the Publisher.

How To Use This Study Guide

This five-lesson study guide corresponds to *"The Fire of God in Your Life" With Rick Renner* (**Renner TV**). Each lesson in this study guide covers a topic that is addressed during the program series, with questions and references supplied to draw you deeper into your own private study of the Scriptures on this subject.

To derive the most benefit from this study guide, consider the following:

First, watch or listen to the program prior to working through the corresponding lesson in this guide. (Programs can also be viewed at **renner.org** by clicking on the Media/Archives links or on our Renner Ministries YouTube channel.)

Second, take the time to look up the scriptures included in each lesson. Prayerfully consider their application to your own life.

Third, use a journal or notebook to make note of your answers to each lesson's Study Questions and Practical Application challenges.

Fourth, invest specific time in prayer and in the Word of God to consult with the Holy Spirit. Write down the scriptures or insights He reveals to you.

Finally, take action! Whatever the Lord tells you to do according to His Word, do it.

For added insights on this subject, it is recommended that you obtain Rick Renner's book *A Life Ablaze*. You may also select from Rick's other available resources by placing your order at **renner.org** or by calling 1-800-742-5593.

LESSON 1

TOPIC

Fire Removes Excess Waste and Makes You Stronger

SCRIPTURES

1. **1 Thessalonians 2:4** — But as we were allowed of God to be put in trust with the gospel, even so we speak; not as pleasing men, but God, which trieth our hearts.

GREEK WORDS

1. "allowed" — δοκιμάζω (*dokimadzo*): to test; to examine; to inspect; to scrutinize; to determine the quality or sincerity of a thing; the object scrutinized has passed the test, so it can now be viewed as genuine and sincere; this word δοκιμάζω (*dokimadzo*) was used to illustrate the test used to determine real and counterfeit coinage; after a scrutinizing test was performed, the bona fide coinage would stand up to the test and the counterfeit would fail; this word δοκιμάζω (*dokimadzo*) was used to picture the refining of metal by fire to remove its impurities; first, the metal was placed in a fire that burned at a certain degree of heat; then, it was placed in a fire burning at an even higher degree; and finally, it was placed in a blazing fire that burned at the highest degree of all; three such tests were needed in order to remove from the metal all the unseen impurities that were hidden from the naked eye; from the viewpoint of the naked eye, the metal probably looked strong and ready to be used even prior to those tests, but unseen defects were resident in the metal that would have shown up later as a break, fracture, or some kind of malfunction; before a person could be assured that the metal was free of defects and thus ready to be used, these three purifying tests at three different degrees of blazing hot fire were required; the fire was hot and the process was lengthy, but the tests were necessary in order to achieve a good product
2. "of" God — ὑπὸ (*hupo*): by; directly by; under; under the guidance of

SYNOPSIS

The five lessons in this study, *The Fire of God in Your Life*, will focus on the following topics:

- Fire Removes Excess Waste and Makes You Stronger
- Fire Reveals Flaws That Need To Be Corrected
- Fire Is Needed To Make Your Life Shine
- Fire Brings Color to Your Life
- Fire Is Required if You Want To Have Gold in Your Life

The emphasis of this lesson:

The fiery presence of God is required to remove excess from our life and make us strong for what He has called us to do. It is the fire of God that makes us durable and unbreakable. Rather than run from God's season of fiery preparation, we need to embrace it so that we're ready for the task at hand.

Just outside the city of Moscow is the town of Gzhel, which is known for its extraordinary Russian porcelain. Today, there are five factories that produce these vessels, which are used all over the world. The process begins when a master craftsman creates a unique and amazing piece, and a mold of that piece is then manufactured.

Other craftsmen then take the mold and pour liquid clay into it, forming a duplicate of the original masterpiece. The newly formed piece then sits in the mold for about 30 minutes to dry after which it is removed and the work on it continues. For example, handles are often attached at this point. The various pieces are inserted into each other by the craftsman, and once they are finished assembling all the pieces of the vessel, it will be taken to the oven for the first firing.

At this point in the creative process, the assembled piece is so soft and fragile it cannot be held by its handle, or it will break. Instead, the vessel must be fully supported from the bottom and gently placed in the oven. It is the fire of the oven that makes the piece strong. Without the fire, the vessel is weak.

Once it has been placed into the oven, the temperature will gradually be increased until it reaches 900 degrees. For 24 hours, the vessel will be kept in the fire, and then it will be removed. The time spent in the fire toughens the clay vessel, making it durable and no longer breakable. Now it is strong and ready to be taken to the next level of development.

This process is very similar to the way God works in our life. He pours Himself into us, preparing us to take on the form of His Son, Jesus. The Holy Spirit continues to work with us, cutting off all the unneeded excess in our lives. Little by little, He reveals and deals with our flaws and removes the unnecessary baggage from our past that is weighing us down.

He then turns up the heat, allowing us to go through fiery trials. Although we all look for ways to escape the fire, it is the fire of God in our lives that produces benefits that can be found nowhere else. Friend, we need the fire of God in our life!

What Would the World Be Like Without Fire?

Have you ever stopped to think about what life would be like without fire? It is a sobering thought indeed. In his book *A Life Ablaze*, Rick explores this idea of life without fire. He wrote:

> Life would be very primitive. Without fire, humankind would only have the moon and stars as a light source at night. For early humans, fire was essential to extend the day, provide heat, ward off predators and insects, illuminate dark places, and facilitate cooking. Long before gas and electricity were invented, people totally depended on fire for light, for heat, and for *survival*.
>
> Without fire, there is no light in the dark, no heat in winter, no cooking of meat or baking of bread, no burning of bricks, no smelting of ore — basically, no civilization. The discovery of fire was one of the greatest discoveries ever made in humanity, and we can't imagine life *without* fire. Fire was needed to create tools and to make weapons, and the energy produced by fire was essential for constructing buildings and making machines fueled by the engines of the Industrial Revolution. Finally, fire determined the outcome of two world wars and the ultimate emergence of superpowers in the geopolitical realm.
>
> Today we still use fire to create technology and to make the world a more comfortable place to live. Fire still burns coal and oil to make electricity. In fact, if we were to remove fire from the world,

life would be similar to living on the moon! There would be no electricity, no warmth, and no cooked food. Shelter, agriculture, and technology in general would not be able to progress without fire. Without fire, technology would be impossible to create. Metal is shaped to make wires and phones by the use of heat derived from fire. Without metal, no electricity could be transported to facilitate a host of functions needed to keep civilization running.

Fire! We must have it for survival, for development, and for progress. Likewise, we must have *spiritual fire* if we are to move forward in the advancement of God's purposes and in the fulfillment of His great plan![1]

Are you beginning to see the immense importance of fire — and why we need spiritual fire in our lives? Not only is it necessary for survival, but also for progress and the ability to advance in the tasks God has assigned to us.

The Apostle Paul Was Familiar With Fire

The apostle Paul was no stranger to the fire of God. He was subjected to heated trials again and again in order to be prepared for ministry. At times, he must have wondered, *Will the day ever come when I'm finally launched into the ministry Jesus called me to?* Yet, it was during that season of waiting that God was removing imperfections and weaknesses from Paul's life and strengthening him to be ready for ministry.

Acts 9:20-25 documents that when Paul was first saved, he immediately tried to enter public ministry. It seems he thought that because he had such a high ranking among the Jews, he ought to immediately have a high ranking among the apostles. This arrogant attitude caused him to make quite a stir wherever he went, so much so that the Jews and Greeks alike were watching and waiting for an opportunity to kill Paul. Although he had a powerful revelation of Christ, he lacked the spiritual maturity needed to be in leadership.

To help Paul grow up spiritually, God brought him through a process of preparation. Paul speaks of this in First Thessalonians 2:4 where he says, "But as we were allowed of God to be put in trust with the gospel, even so we speak; not as pleasing men, but God, which trieth our hearts."

The word "allowed" in this verse is a poor translation of the original text. In Greek, it is the word *dokimadzo*, which means *to test*, *to examine*, *to inspect*, or *to scrutinize*. It was a term used to determine the quality or sincerity of a thing, and once the object scrutinized had passed the test, it was now viewed as genuine and sincere. Specifically, *dokimadzo* was used to illustrate the test used to determine real and counterfeit coinage; after a scrutinizing test by fire was performed, the bona fide coinage would stand up to the test and the counterfeit would fail.

Interestingly, this word *dokimadzo* was also used to picture the refining of metal by fire to remove its impurities. First, the metal was placed in a fire that burned at a certain degree of heat; then, it was placed in a fire burning at an even higher degree. Finally, it was placed in a blazing fire that burned at the highest degree of all. Thus, three such tests were needed in order to remove from the metal all the unseen impurities that were hidden from the naked eye. Although the metal probably looked strong and ready to be used even prior to those tests, unseen defects were resident in the metal that would have shown up later as a break, fracture, or some kind of malfunction. Therefore, before a person could be assured that the metal was free of defects and ready to be used, these three purifying tests at three different degrees of blazing hot fire were required. The fire was hot, and the process was lengthy, but the tests were necessary in order to achieve a good product.

Amazingly, it is this same word *dokimadzo* — translated here as "allowed" — that Paul used to describe what he went through in order to be entrusted with ministering the Gospel. Basically, he is saying, "God put me through three intense levels of blazing fire to get me ready." And this testing, Paul said, was "of God." The word "of" here is the Greek word *hupo*, which means *by*, *directly by*, *under*, or *under the guidance of*. Thus, Paul is telling us that the refinement of his life was applied *directly by God* and *under His guidance*.

Paul went on to say, "…Even so we speak; not as pleasing men, but God, which trieth our hearts" (1 Thessalonians 2:4). The word "trieth" is again the Greek word *dokimadzo*, but here it is in a continuous sense, which indicates not only did Paul and his ministry associates go through fire in the past, they were also being tested regularly by God to prepare them for future advancements.

Taking into account the original Greek meanings, here is the *Renner Interpretive Version (RIV)* of First Thessalonians 2:4:

It was a lengthy process, and I went through a lot of refining fires to get to this place, but I finally passed the test, and God saw that I was genuinely ready…and it's not over because God is still testing our hearts to see if we're ready for the next big step.

What Was Paul's First 'Oven' of Preparation?

The Bible and Early Church history inform us that God placed Paul in the church of Antioch where he served alongside four other leaders whom he probably thought were inferior to him. Of the five, Paul was the only theologian among them, and in the eight years that he served with those other four leaders, Paul had to learn humility, which was a new way of living for him.

During those eight years in Antioch, there must have been moments when Paul thought, *God, how long do I have to put up with all the ignorance around me?* Nevertheless, God was using the people and environment of Antioch to deal with Paul's character. Antioch served as the refiner's fire that prepared Paul for ministry. God was removing things from Paul's life that later would have hurt him or hurt others, all the while making him spiritually strong and prepared to minister effectively.

Although many Christians are clock-watchers, God is a character-watcher. He's looking at our character to see if we have the needed maturity for what He's prepared for us to do, and He uses fire to prepare us. He allows the heat to be turned up in our lives in order to expose and remove things that would embarrass and discredit us or possibly hurt others. Why? Because He loves us and wants us to be ready for what we've been waiting to do.

STUDY QUESTIONS

> Study to shew thyself approved unto God, a workman that needeth not to be ashamed, rightly dividing the word of truth.
> — 2 Timothy 2:15

1. As we learned in today's lesson, one of the ways fire is used is to purify metal — to make it usable for building, so that whatever the metal is used for, it's proven to be strong, solid, and unbreakable. What do you think would happen if metal was NOT tested by fire, but then

that metal was used in the construction of bridges, skyscrapers, and buildings? How do you think this applies to the development of your character?

2. According to Jeremiah 23:29, what is the most important and powerful form of "fire" that God desires to use to refine and purify your life? What does God say you can expect to happen when you consistently embrace this fire? (*See* Psalm 119:9; Hebrews 4:12; John 8:31,32; and James 1:21-25.)

PRACTICAL APPLICATION

> But be ye doers of the word, and not hearers only, deceiving your own selves.
> —James 1:22

Metal that has been tested in the fire can be trusted as *reliable*. If it is untested, it is *unreliable*. The same can be said of people. An unreliable person isn't just someone who's learning and makes mistakes at times — we all do because we're human. It's someone who just doesn't take their job seriously at all, or maybe was promoted too quickly to a position they weren't equipped to handle.

1. Have you ever had to work with an unreliable person? What was it like? What does Scripture say about unreliability? (*See* Proverbs 25:14 and 19.)
2. On the flip side, have you ever worked with someone who was reliable and ready for anything your team needed to tackle? What was it like to work with that person? What do you most appreciate about their attitude and efforts? What do Proverbs 13:17 and 25:13 say about how reliability affects others?
3. Are there any ways you want to grow in reliability? Take some time and ask God to help you cooperate with His refining process so you can become a solid, reliable vessel for Him to work through.

---

[1] Rick Renner, *A Life Ablaze: Ten Simple Keys To Living on Fire for God* (Shippensburg, PA: Harrison House, 2020), pp. 23-24.

LESSON 2

TOPIC
Fire Reveals Flaws That Need To Be Corrected

SCRIPTURES
1. **1 Thessalonians 2:4** — But as we were allowed of God to be put in trust with the gospel, even so we speak; not as pleasing men, but God, which trieth our hearts.

GREEK WORDS
1. "allowed" — δοκιμάζω (*dokimadzo*): to test; to examine; to inspect; to scrutinize; to determine the quality or sincerity of a thing; the object scrutinized has passed the test, so it can now be viewed as genuine and sincere; this word δοκιμάζω (*dokimadzo*) was used to illustrate the test used to determine real and counterfeit coinage; after a scrutinizing test was performed, the bona fide coinage would stand up to the test and the counterfeit would fail; this word δοκιμάζω (*dokimadzo*) was used to picture the refining of metal by fire to remove its impurities; first, the metal was placed in a fire that burned at a certain degree of heat; then, it was placed in a fire burning at an even higher degree; and finally, it was placed in a blazing fire that burned at the highest degree of all; three such tests were needed in order to remove from the metal all the unseen impurities that were hidden from the naked eye; from the viewpoint of the naked eye, the metal probably looked strong and ready to be used even prior to those tests, but unseen defects were resident in the metal that would have shown up later as a break, fracture, or some kind of malfunction; before a person could be assured that the metal was free of defects and thus ready to be used, these three purifying tests at three different degrees of blazing hot fire were required; the fire was hot and the process was lengthy, but the tests were necessary in order to achieve a good product

2. "of" God — ὑπὸ (*hupo*): by; directly by; under; under the guidance of

3. "trieth" — δοκιμάζω (*dokimadzo*): a form of the same word, but here in a continuous sense

SYNOPSIS

As we noted in Lesson 1, Russian Gzhel is simply magnificent. But before it becomes the classic blue and white porcelain that people have come to know and love, it must go through a tedious process of development. First, liquid clay is poured into a mold, and after a short time, it is removed from the mold and the excess material is cut off. Handles, or other intricate pieces created to adorn the vessel, are then attached just before it is placed into an oven for a 24-hour stay in 900-degree heat.

The result of this first degree of intense fire is that the vessel has shrunk as much as 15 percent. It is then checked for any defects by dipping it into a special chemical solution. If there are any imperfections in the piece, the chemical solution is designed to reveal them once it's pulled out. If fractures or flaws are present when the craftsmen pull the piece out of the solution, they cannot proceed until they determine how to fix them. Thus, they begin to work on removing all imperfections by chipping away at every little nick.

Once the vessel is corrected, a special glaze is applied around all the critical pieces to ensure there are no more defects or fractures. When a piece has been confirmed to be free of flaws, the master craftsman officially marks the piece as *approved* with a green stamp on the bottom. This seal of approval means that the piece is complete and ready to go to the next phase.

This is very similar to what God does in our life. The Bible says, "The steps of a [good] man are directed and established by the Lord when He delights in his way [and He busies Himself with his every step]" (Psalm 37:23 *AMPC*). With every step, God serves as the Master Craftsman, checking us to make sure we're progressing into wholeness. If there are any defects or cracks that need to be fixed, His Spirit swings into action repairing what is out of order. All of this is a part of God's work in our life.

The emphasis of this lesson:

When God puts you in the right environment, His fire exposes the defects in your life. In His mercy and kindness, He lovingly works to remove the flaws and weaknesses so that you are ready to advance to the next phase of His plan for you.

Paul Was 'Allowed of God' To Be Put in Trust With the Gospel

In First Thessalonians 2:4, the apostle Paul wrote, "But as we were allowed of God to be put in trust with the gospel, even so we speak; not as pleasing men, but God, which trieth our hearts." In Lesson 1, we saw that the word "allowed" is an inaccurate translation of the original text. In Greek, it is the word *dokimadzo*, which means *to test, to examine, to inspect,* or *to scrutinize.*

This means we could translate Paul's words as, "…We were tested of God," "…We were examined of God," "…We were inspected of God," or "…We were scrutinized of God." Just like newly formed Russian porcelain is placed in the fire and then dipped into a chemical bath to reveal any flaws, God tested Paul — and He tests us — to determine if we're ready for the next phase.

The word *dokimadzo* — translated here as "allowed" — was used to determine the quality or sincerity of a thing, and once the object scrutinized had passed the test, it was viewed as genuine and sincere. For instance, *dokimadzo* was used to illustrate the test used to determine if coins were real or counterfeit. After a scrutinizing test was performed, the bona fide coinage would stand up to the test of fire, and the counterfeit would fail.

Furthermore, this word *dokimadzo* was also used to picture the refining of metal by fire to remove its impurities. First, the metal was placed in a fire that burned at a certain degree of heat; then, it was placed in a fire burning at an even higher degree. Finally, it was placed in a blazing fire that burned at the highest degree of all. Thus, three different degrees of fire were needed to remove all the unseen impurities from the metal that were hidden from the naked eye. The final phase of this process is where we get the idea of *putting someone through the third degree.*

Now, to the naked eye, the metal probably looks strong and ready to be used even prior to those tests. However, unseen defects were resident in the metal that would have shown up later as a break, fracture, or some kind of malfunction. Therefore, before a person could be assured that the metal was free of defects and ready to be used for construction, these three purifying tests at three different degrees of blazing hot fire were required. The fire was hot, and the process was lengthy. Still, the tests were necessary in order to achieve a good, reliable product.

Interestingly, when Paul said he and his associates were "allowed" of God to be entrusted with the Gospel, he used the word *dokimadzo*. It was his way of saying, "God put us through three degrees of heat to get us ready for ministry." There was so much in Paul's character that needed to be changed when he first got saved that God subjected him to intense fiery testing. And this testing, Paul said, was "of God." The word "of" here is the Greek word *hupo*, which means *by, directly by, under,* or *under the guidance of.* Thus, Paul is telling us that God Himself was overseeing the refinement process of his life.

Paul went on to say, "…Even so we speak; not as pleasing men, but God, which trieth our hearts" (1 Thessalonians 2:4). The word "trieth" here is again the Greek word *dokimadzo*, but in this instance, it is in a continuous sense, which means the testing process never ends. In addition to the initial time of testing, Paul and his ministry companions were being tested continually by God to prepare them for future advancements.

Taking into account the original Greek meanings, here is the *Renner Interpretive Version (RIV)* of First Thessalonians 2:4:

> **It was a lengthy process, and I went through a lot of refining fires to get to this place, but I finally passed the test, and God saw that I was genuinely ready…and it's not over because God is still testing our hearts to see if we're ready for the next big step.**

Saul Was Convinced He Could Lead, But He Was Far From Ready

In Acts 9, we find the historical account of Paul's life-changing encounter with Christ on the road to Damascus. Toward the end of the chapter, the Bible tells us that immediately after Paul's conversion he began to preach the Good News in the synagogues of Damascus (*see* vv. 19-25). From there, he went and did the same thing in Jerusalem.

Acts 9:26 says, "And when Saul was come to Jerusalem, he assayed to join himself to the disciples: but they were all afraid of him, and believed not that he was a disciple." Here we find that Paul — then known as Saul — had a very serious flaw in his character. Although he was saved and serving Jesus, he was prideful. Before coming to Christ, he held a position of great prestige among the Jews. It seems that immediately after becoming a Christian, he assumed he held the same high ranking among Christians — so much so that he tried to join himself to the apostles as their equal!

The Bible also says that the believers in Jerusalem were afraid of Paul, and the reason for their fear was because his character was so raw. Nevertheless, there was one man who believed in Paul, and that was Barnabas. It was Barnabas who could see the gift of God in Paul's life, and the Bible says:

> **But Barnabas took him, and brought him to the apostles, and declared unto them how he had seen the Lord in the way, and that he had spoken to him, and how he had preached boldly at Damascus in the name of Jesus. And he was with them coming in and going out at Jerusalem. And he spake boldly in the name of the Lord Jesus, and disputed against the Grecians: but they went about to slay him.**
>
> — Acts 9:27-29

Without question, Paul was anointed by God to teach and preach about Jesus, and he certainly had an apostolic call on his life. However, he was not ready to be launched into apostolic ministry immediately after being saved. His inexperience and unbridled efforts caused many Jews and Gentiles alike to seek to kill him. Acts 9:30 says, "…When the brethren knew [that Paul's life was in jeopardy], they brought him down to Caesarea, and sent him forth to Tarsus."

This verse lets us know several things. First, it is apparent that the apostles in Jerusalem were initially unaware of Paul's actions, which means Paul was not operating under God's established authority, nor was he submitted to their training. When the spiritual leaders of the Church learned how out of control Paul was, they put him on a boat and sent him on a one-way trip back to his hometown of Tarsus. How long was Paul absent from the Church scene? The Bible doesn't say. But we do know he was gone for quite some time, and there is no scriptural evidence that he was looking to return.

The Sovereignty of God
Helped To Prepare Paul for Ministry

Meanwhile, a watershed moment took place in Acts 10. God in His sovereignty began pouring out His Spirit upon the Gentiles, selecting Cornelius and his family to be the first to be saved and baptized in the Spirit. At the same time, the Bible says a great number of Gentiles turned to the Lord in the city of Antioch. In fact, the grace of God was moving so powerfully, the apostles sent Barnabas to assist in the ministry there.

After seeing the unprecedented move of God in Antioch, the Bible says, "Then departed Barnabas to Tarsus, for to seek Saul: And when he had found him, he brought him unto Antioch. And it came to pass, that a whole year they assembled themselves with the church, and taught much people…" (Acts 11:25,26).

We don't hear anything else about Paul until Acts 13 where the Bible says, "Now there were in the church that was at Antioch certain prophets and teachers; as Barnabas, and Simeon that was called Niger, and Lucius of Cyrene, and Manaen, which had been brought up with Herod the tetrarch, and Saul. As they ministered to the Lord, and fasted, the Holy Ghost said, Separate me Barnabas and Saul for the work whereunto I have called them" (Acts 13:1,2).

Although it may seem these events unfolded rather quickly, they did not. In fact, Early Church history tells us that Paul served side by side as a co-equal leader with these men for about eight years. That's a long time! And it's far from the impression most of us have of Paul: that he got saved and immediately launched into his ministry. Instead, he was placed into the church of Antioch by God Himself. This environment served as Paul's "oven" where the fire of God revealed his flaws and defects — and where Paul learned the crucial skill of how to submit to authority and respect others.

Think about it: If Paul would have remained in Jerusalem, God probably couldn't have dealt with the pride in Paul's life. After all, Paul was a Jewish theologian, and in Jerusalem, he would have seen himself as the leader of leaders. But God moved him 250 miles away to the city of Antioch, into a Gentile church, which was a fiery experience in itself because he had never had much interaction with Gentiles. Moreover, because the people serving with him in leadership as teachers and prophets were not theologically trained, Paul had to learn how to respect those who had gifts and backgrounds that were different from his own. He had to learn how to see himself as one who was co-equal with other leaders. He had to learn how to submit to authority, and for eight years he was in the "cooker" as God prepared him. There must have been moments when Paul thought, *God how long is this going to last?*

You see, Paul had a revelation of Christ, but he didn't really have a relationship with the body of Christ. And in those eight years in the "oven" of Antioch, God was refining him, God was preparing him, and God was teaching him. Even though he may have at times wanted to escape the fire, God would not let him out of the oven because that heat was necessary for his preparation.

STUDY QUESTIONS

> Study to shew thyself approved unto God, a workman that needeth not to be ashamed, rightly dividing the word of truth.
> — 2 Timothy 2:15

A primary reason for putting metal or a clay vessel through fire is to remove its impurities. In the same way, the fire of God infuses us with strength and purifies us as His vessel.

1. What did Paul tell Timothy, his spiritual son, about the importance of *purity* in Second Timothy 2:20-22? How does purity affect your availability and usefulness in God's hands?

2. Take a moment to pray and ask God, *What impurities are You in the process of removing from my life right now? Please give me the grace to lean into You and cooperate with what You're doing so the work can be fully completed. In Jesus' name. Amen.*

3. Now take time to write down whatever God is showing you about the purpose of the current fire you're in, and take hope in the fact that He's promised to complete all the work He's doing in you (*see* Philippians 1:6 and 1 Thessalonians 5:23,24).

PRACTICAL APPLICATION

> But be ye doers of the word, and not hearers only, deceiving your own selves.
> — James 1:22

Abraham is one of the first examples in Scripture of people experiencing the fire of God. The fact that God instructed him to leave his family and everything he knew and go to a land God would show him exposed him to the fire of uncertainty and isolation.

1. Have you ever found yourself feeling *alone* or *uncertain* as you were following God's instructions? If that's where you find yourself now, pray and tell Him what's going on in your heart and mind.
2. God also promised Abraham that he and Sarah would have a son that would be an heir to all his promises (*see* Genesis 15:1-6; 18:10-14). The son that God spoke of wasn't born for another 25 years. What is something that God has either promised you or given you a deep desire for that just hasn't happened yet? How long have you been waiting?
3. God knows that when our hopes are deferred, it makes our hearts sick (*see* Proverbs 13:12). What encouragement does He provide you in Psalm 34:18 and 145:13-19?
4. Unexpected delays are prolonged fires. They tend to either force us *away from God* in bitterness and frustration or *toward Him* in brokenness and openness. Which way have you allowed your fires to push you? Take a few minutes to talk to God and invite Him to redeem the chapters of your story that you thought would end your purpose. Watch for the ways He starts to heal you and give you fresh vision for what He has ahead.

LESSON 3

TOPIC

Fire Is Needed To Make Your Light Shine

SCRIPTURES

1. **1 Thessalonians 2:4** — But as we were allowed of God to be put in trust with the gospel, even so we speak; not as pleasing men, but God, which trieth our hearts.

GREEK WORDS

1. "allowed" — δοκιμάζω (*dokimadzo*): to test; to examine; to inspect; to scrutinize; to determine the quality or sincerity of a thing; the object scrutinized has passed the test, so it can now be viewed as genuine and sincere; this word δοκιμάζω (*dokimadzo*) was used to illustrate the test used to determine real and counterfeit coinage; after a scrutinizing test was performed, the bona fide coinage would stand up to the test and the counterfeit would fail; this word δοκιμάζω (*dokimadzo*) was used to picture the refining of metal by fire to remove its impurities; first, the metal was placed in a fire that burned at a certain degree of heat; then, it was placed in a fire burning at an even higher degree; and finally, it was placed in a blazing fire that burned at the highest degree of all; three such tests were needed in order to remove from the metal all the unseen impurities that were hidden from the naked eye; from the viewpoint of the naked eye, the metal probably looked strong and ready to be used even prior to those tests, but unseen defects were resident in the metal that would have shown up later as a break, fracture, or some kind of malfunction; before a person could be assured that the metal was free of defects and thus ready to be used, these three purifying tests at three different degrees of blazing hot fire were required; the fire was hot and the process was lengthy, but the tests were necessary in order to achieve a good product
2. "of" God — ὑπὸ (*hupo*): by; directly by; under; under the guidance of
3. "trieth" — δοκιμάζω (*dokimadzo*): a form of the same word, but here in a continuous sense

SYNOPSIS

In Lesson 2, we saw that once a piece of Russian Gzhel has been confirmed to be free of flaws, it is officially approved, and a green stamp is placed on its bottom by the master craftsman. This seal of approval means that the piece is complete and ready to go to the next phase, which is to be hand-painted by master artists.

As strange as it may seem, Russian Gzhel doesn't start out as the beautiful blue and white treasure people love. It begins as a plain piece of porcelain painted with black and white cobalt paint. Once painted, the vessel is transported to a room where it is submerged in a special glaze. Although you can no longer see what is under the glaze, the dull, black and white paint is transformed into the vibrant blue and white hues it's known for once it is placed into the fire. The fire brings the colors to life, and the glaze makes the piece gleam and shine.

In many ways, this is what happens in our life. God is doing a wonderful work in us, but we cannot really see it. It's as if we are covered by a thick layer of glaze, and the beauty of who we are in Christ is hidden from us and public view. That's where the fire of God comes in. When God brings His fire into our lives, it tests us, purifies us, and adds brilliant color and makes us shine brightly in the dark world around us. Friend, if your life is dull and colorless, you need to embrace the fire of God!

The emphasis of this lesson:

The environment of the church in Antioch served as a refining fire to incinerate the impurities of pride and prejudice in Paul's heart. It was in Antioch that he learned how to submit to the authority of others and received the revelation of the new man in Christ. God used Paul's gifts to cultivate the gifts in others.

A Review of Our Anchor Verse
First Thessalonians 2:4

The word "allowed" means *to test, to examine, to inspect,* or *to scrutinize*.

When we look at First Thessalonians 2:4, the apostle Paul gives us his personal testimony of the fire of God at work in his life. He said, "But as we were allowed of God to be put in trust with the gospel, even so we speak; not as pleasing men, but God, which trieth our hearts." It's interesting to note that the words "allowed" and "trieth" are from the same Greek word. It is the word *dokimadzo*, which means *to test, to examine, to inspect,* or *to scrutinize*.

The use of *dokimadzo* means we could translate Paul's words as, "…We were *tested* of God," "…We were *examined* of God," "…We were *inspected* of God," or "…We were *scrutinized* of God." The word *dokimadzo* also described a test that was used to determine the quality or sincerity of a thing. Once the object being tested finally passed the test, it was viewed as genuine, sincere, and ready for use.

We've also noted that the term *dokimadzo* was used to illustrate the test to determine if coins were real or counterfeit. After a scrutinizing test of fire was performed on the coins, the bona fide coinage would stand up to the test, but the counterfeit would fail.

God uses fiery tests to burn the impurities out of our life.

Most importantly, this word *dokimadzo* was also used to picture the refining of metal by fire to remove its impurities. First, the metal was placed in a fire that burned at a certain degree of heat; the fire caused the impurities in the metal to separate and rise to the top. The refiner would then scrape off the impurities with a special tool. Then the metal was placed in another fire burning at an even higher degree. Once the refiner scraped off the impurities that surfaced, the metal was placed in a third fire that burned at the highest degree of all. Thus, this metal was placed into three different degrees of fire in order to remove all the unseen impurities that were hidden from the naked eye. This is where we get the idea of *putting someone through the third degree*.

Of course, to the naked eye, this metal probably looked strong and ready to be used even prior to these tests. However, unseen defects were resident in the metal that would have shown up later as a break, fracture, or some kind of malfunction. Thus, before a person could be assured that the metal was free of defects and ready to be used, these three purifying tests at three varying degrees of blazing hot fire were required. The fire was hot, and the process was lengthy. Yet, the tests were necessary in order to achieve a good, reliable product.

All tests we experience are directly under God's guidance.

Paul said the testing and scrutinizing he experienced was "of God." The word "of" here is the Greek word *hupo*, which means *by*, *directly by*, *under*, or *under the guidance of*. The inclusion of the word *hupo* tells us that God was the One who was orchestrating Paul's purification. He was the One who put Paul into the varying degrees of blazing fire over a number of years to expose and remove the impurities in his character that later would have shown up as a fracture or a flaw that could have injured others or severely damaged their spiritual growth.

Can you think of people in ministry who failed because they were promoted too quickly? Although they were called by God, they had character flaws in their life that were never corrected. Later, when they were serving in public ministry and the pressure became too great, those character flaws manifested as serious problems — problems that could have been eliminated from their life had they stayed in the fire of God a little longer.

Paul went on to say, "…Even so we speak; not as pleasing men, but God, which trieth our hearts" (1 Thessalonians 2:4). The word "trieth" here is again the Greek word *dokimadzo*, but in this case it is in a continuous sense, which means the fiery tests never end. Although none of us like the preparation process, we need to learn to embrace it because God is always preparing us for future advancements.

Taking into account the original Greek meanings, here is the *Renner Interpretive Version (RIV)* of First Thessalonians 2:4:

> **It was a lengthy process, and I went through a lot of refining fires to get to this place, but I finally passed the test, and God saw that I was genuinely ready…and it's not over because God is still testing our hearts to see if we're ready for the next big step.**

Antioch Was a Place of Testing for Paul

When Paul encountered Jesus on the road to Damascus and surrendered his life to Him, he was immediately saved and called into ministry. However, there were issues in his life — especially pride and deep-seated prejudice — that needed to be exposed and eliminated before he could be launched into ministry. God loved Paul and the newly emerging Church so much that He placed Paul in the church of Antioch to test him and prepare him for ministry.

In Acts 13:1, we learn about the leadership team at Antioch. It says, "Now there were in the church that was at Antioch certain prophets and teachers; as Barnabas, and Simeon that was called Niger, and Lucius of Cyrene, and Manaen, which had been brought up with Herod the tetrarch, and Saul." In this verse, five men are mentioned and listed as co-leaders at the church in Antioch.

The leaders of the church in Antioch:

Barnabas is listed first. He was a Levite from the Gentile country of Cyprus, which was a region in Greece (*see* Acts 4:36). He was a distant Jew descended from the tribe of Levi. Because he was raised so far from

Jerusalem, it is likely that he didn't grow up around the strict religious environment that was so characteristic of that city.

Simeon is listed second and is referred to as "Niger," which is the Latin word meaning *black*. Scholars speculate that this indicates Simeon was probably a black man from Africa and may have even been the slave of a Roman family at some point earlier in his life. Regardless, he served in a position of authority in the church of Antioch.

Lucius of Cyrene is third in the lineup. Cyrene was a region in Northern Africa, and some speculate this may have been Luke, which seems unlikely. Others argue that Lucius was a man of North African heritage. The name "Lucius" actually means *light* or *bright*. Regardless of the identity of this man, it seems he had come to Antioch from Northern Africa.

Manaen is co-leader number four. He had been brought up with Herod the tetrarch and was, in fact, probably a relative of the family of Herod, which means he was a pagan as he was growing up. Because Manaen was Roman and likely descended from the royal family, he received a Roman education. This is especially significant because educated Romans were raised to look down on foreigners as being uncouth barbarians who were classed as "less" than Romans. Manaen's position, alongside other ethnicities and skin colors, lets us know that he had broken free from the prejudices of his upbringing to work alongside two Africans and two Jews who were brothers in the Lord.

Paul — who was called Saul at that time — is the fifth co-leader mentioned. He was born into a very well-connected, tremendously wealthy Jewish family who were also Roman citizens. Being raised in a wealthy home, Saul was afforded the best education money could buy. He was also theologically trained for his former position as a rabbi and Pharisee. Consequently, Saul was the most religiously instructed and possessed the greatest breadth of scriptural knowledge of any of his co-leaders in Antioch.

Stop and take a good look at this group of men Paul was with. One of them, Barnabas, was a Jew. Two of them — Lucius and Simeon, one who was possibly a former slave — were dark-skinned Africans. And Manaen was a pagan from Rome who got saved. Only God could put together such an against-the-odds arrangement of people! Indeed, this multiracial group and environment in Antioch broke all societal norms, but it was the perfect proving ground for Paul to be tested and prepared for ministry.

Paul Received the Revelation of the New Man in Antioch

Keep in mind that as a Jew, Saul (who became the apostle Paul) had been raised to believe he was to have no contact with Gentiles. In fact, he was taught to see himself as being better than Gentiles. Yet God had him serving as a co-equal leader with three Gentiles. This was unthinkable to Saul, not to mention the challenges of working alongside all four of these co-leaders who weren't even remotely theologically trained.

It was in the "oven" of Antioch that God began to deal with Saul's issues of pride and prejudice, bringing him to the realization that *God loves everyone* and *works through everyone with a willing, humble heart*. It was in the fire of testing of Antioch that Saul became Paul and received the divine revelation of the new man in Christ, which he wrote about in Galatians and Colossians:

> **There is neither Jew nor Greek, there is neither bond nor free, there is neither male nor female: for ye are all one in Christ Jesus.**
>
> **— Galatians 3:28**

> **...Put on the new man, which is renewed in knowledge after the image of him that created him: Where there is neither Greek nor Jew, circumcision nor uncircumcision, Barbarian, Scythian, bond nor free: but Christ is all, and in all.**
>
> **— Colossians 3:10,11**

As we noted, Saul served in Antioch for eight years, and it was during that season he also learned how to submit to the authority of others. Although he was more theologically trained than anyone else in the group, God had *not* placed him over the others. They were co-leaders, and each of them brought something valuable to the table. There may have been times when Saul thought, *Why in the world am I sitting as a co-equal with these others? I have more spiritual knowledge and revelation than all of them.* But God had put him there to serve alongside the others for a purpose, and as time passed, he would discover it.

God Used Paul's Gifts
To Cultivate the Gifts in Others

In addition to God refining Saul's character and removing the deadly defects of arrogance and immaturity, God used him to cultivate and sharpen the gifts in others. He provided his co-leaders and the congregation of Antioch with a solid foundation of the Word of God. His years of study and Jewish heritage provided him with a wealth of knowledge. Having him on their teaching staff gave all the believers in Antioch unprecedented access to an expert on Jewish culture and the Old Testament. As a trained rabbi and theologian, Saul was like a fish in water when it came to the subject of creation, the Old Testament covenants, Messianic prophecies, Jesus' lineage, the Shekinah glory of God, and simple Jewish history. This was Saul's niche in Antioch, and God used his gifts to effectively grow and mature His Church.

At the same time Saul was giving out to others, he was also taking in a powerful picture of what the Church should look like — a colorful tapestry of people from all walks of life. In Antioch, blacks, whites, Jews, and Gentiles all mingled together in leadership and worship, which was something that had never existed before. God used the plethora of nationalities and cultures represented in the congregation to give Saul a broad perspective of the new man in Christ and the Gospel and its mission.

He saw with his own eyes the power of God working in and through people of all nations. How could he argue with a Greek being saved or an African being a leader in the church? All these amazing things were happening right in front of him. All this insight and revelation strengthened Saul and added color to his life. The day finally came when God saw that he was ready, and in that moment, the Lord launched him into his ministry — but not until he had embraced the fiery presence of God in his life.

Rick's Experience in the Fire

Paul is not the only Christian leader to go through the fire. The list of people in the Scriptures and throughout history is endless. Rick shared how he, too, entered a time of testing when he first began in the ministry.

> I was a college student and had been studying the Greek New Testament, and I really knew I was called to the ministry. At that

time, I was attending a university church and desperately wanted to launch out and begin teaching. So, I approached the leadership of my church and said, 'You may not know who is in your midst, so let me tell you who I am. I'm called and anointed of God and trained in the knowledge of New Testament Greek. I am the man you need to help set this little church on a good doctrinal foundation, so I'm asking you to give me the opportunity to minister in this church.'

The truth is I was very young and arrogant. To their credit, they wisely said, 'Rick, give us some time to pray and ask the Lord what He would like us to do with you.' Several weeks later, they called me back and said, 'You know, Rick, the Lord said to us that it really is time for your ministry to begin.'

I was so excited! I could hardly wait for them to give me a date when I would begin to teach and to preach. But instead, they said, 'Starting this Saturday, we want you to be responsible for vacuuming all the carpets in the church and setting up the metal folding chairs for services.'

I couldn't believe what I was hearing. I thought, *You're asking me to vacuum carpets and set up chairs? Me — Rick Renner? I'm a gift filled with all kinds of revelation and knowledge.* Nevertheless, vacuuming carpets and setting up chairs was exactly what they asked me to do, so I started doing it. These tasks were God's refining oven for me. He used them to begin dealing with my prideful attitude and to show me that serving in ministry is a privilege. Rather than demand what I wanted, God began to teach me to humble myself and be willing to do anything that was required.

So, as I vacuumed those carpets, which were stained and hard to get clean, I determined in my heart to do the very best I could do. Likewise, as I set up the chairs, I made them as neat and orderly as possible. I even prayed in tongues and asked God to powerfully touch every person that would be sitting in those chairs. I also prayed that the Holy Spirit's presence would fill that place so that people's lives would be forever changed while ministers were teaching — which is what I really wanted to do. Rather than grumbling about and resenting that season of menial tasks, I decided to embrace it, and God released His holy fire to burn out of me the attitudes that needed to go.

Then one day the church elders called me and said, 'Wow! We've been watching you, Rick, and we believe it's time for a promotion.'

Finally! I thought. *They're finally going to ask me to teach!* But what I heard next had absolutely nothing to do with teaching.

'Rick, we want you to be in charge of washing all the dishes in the kitchen.'

Wash dishes? I thought. *Are you really asking me to wash the dishes?* Sure enough, they wanted me to let go of the vacuuming and setting up chairs and take on KP duty. So, with my whole heart, I embraced it. *If washing dishes is what they're asking me,* I said to myself, *I'll clean those dishes to the best of my ability.* Washing dishes was another oven God used to purify and deal with my heart.

The day finally came when the church leaders did indeed ask me to teach. 'We know it's your time, Rick,' they said. Needless to say, I was thrilled and ready to roll, and when they gave me the pulpit for the first time, I was so excited I spoke for an hour and a half! It was finally my pulpit and my time to speak and that's when it all began.

Friend, if God has asked you to do menial things that seem beneath you, don't get angry and complain. Embrace what He's asking you to do! In fact, "Whatever your hand finds to do, do it with all your might…" (Ecclesiastes 9:10 *NKJV*). Remember, God is getting you ready for what He has prepared for you. He's using fiery experiences to remove defects and flaws from your life. Although His correction may seem painful right now, it will produce good fruit and cultivate the maturity you need to succeed in your God-given role and fully enjoy that season when it comes.

STUDY QUESTIONS

> **Study to shew thyself approved unto God, a workman that needeth not to be ashamed, rightly dividing the word of truth.**
> — 2 Timothy 2:15

1. While Paul was in Antioch, he learned to submit to the authority of others, including those who were very different than him. The truth is, before we can be *in* authority, we must first learn how to successfully be *under* authority. Take a few moments to mull over what God says about authority in these verses and write out what the Holy Spirit speaks to you.
   - Romans 13:1,2
   - Exodus 22:28 and Ecclesiastes 10:20
   - 1 Peter 2:13-17
2. One of the purposes for the fire of God is to correct things that are wrong in our lives. According to Hebrews 12:5-13, what two things does God's discipline clearly show us? How does this change your attitude toward it? What are a few blessings you can expect when you embrace the "fire" of His correction?

PRACTICAL APPLICATION

> But be ye doers of the word, and not hearers only, deceiving your own selves.
> —James 1:22

1. Prior to this lesson, what did you know about the apostle Paul's start in ministry? Did you think he began his apostolic work immediately after being saved on the road to Damascus? How does learning that he was initially sent back to Tarsus and then went through eight years of testing in Antioch expand your understanding of his life and God's preparation process?
2. Rick shared about one of his earlier experiences with the fire of God. Can you identify with what he went through? If so, in what ways? What do you sense the Holy Spirit asking you to do to better cooperate with His refining fire in your life?

LESSON 4

TOPIC
Fire Brings Color to Your Life

SCRIPTURES
1. **Thessalonians 2:4** — But as we were allowed of God to be put in trust with the gospel, even so we speak; not as pleasing men, but God, which trieth our hearts.

GREEK WORDS
1. "allowed" — δοκιμάζω (*dokimadzo*): to test; to examine; to inspect; to scrutinize; to determine the quality or sincerity of a thing; the object scrutinized has passed the test, so it can now be viewed as genuine and sincere; this word δοκιμάζω (*dokimadzo*) was used to illustrate the test used to determine real and counterfeit coinage; after a scrutinizing test was performed, the bona fide coinage would stand up to the test and the counterfeit would fail; this word δοκιμάζω (*dokimadzo*) was used to picture the refining of metal by fire to remove its impurities; first, the metal was placed in a fire that burned at a certain degree of heat; then, it was placed in a fire burning at an even higher degree; and finally, it was placed in a blazing fire that burned at the highest degree of all; three such tests were needed in order to remove from the metal all the unseen impurities that were hidden from the naked eye; from the viewpoint of the naked eye, the metal probably looked strong and ready to be used even prior to those tests, but unseen defects were resident in the metal that would have shown up later as a break, fracture, or some kind of malfunction; before a person could be assured that the metal was free of defects and thus ready to be used, these three purifying tests at three different degrees of blazing hot fire were required; the fire was hot and the process was lengthy, but the tests were necessary in order to achieve a good product
2. "of" God — ὑπὸ (*hupo*): by; directly by; under; under the guidance of
3. "trieth" — δοκιμάζω (*dokimadzo*): a form of the same word, but here in a continuous sense

SYNOPSIS

After a piece of Russian Gzhel has been hand-painted and dipped in glaze, it is then moved and placed in another oven. At this point, the Gzhel is so heavy it must be transported in and out of the oven on railroad tracks! This oven is heated to 1,300 degrees — an inferno of fire! It is this most intense heat over 48 hours of time that produces the richest, most exquisite blue and white porcelain treasures that people have come to cherish.

If it feels like you've been going through the fire, don't get discouraged. God is likely at work in your life removing the excess, exposing flaws and defects, and getting you ready for the good things He has prepared for you.

The emphasis of this lesson:

God placed Saul in the unique environment of the church at Antioch to mold and shape him into the person he needed to be to fulfill his destiny. Learning to submit to people so vastly different than himself was a fiery test that brought out the brilliant God-colors in his life. The same will happen in your life as you obey and stay in the environment God placed you.

What We've Learned From First Thessalonians 2:4

Paul was *tested, examined, inspected,* and *scrutinized* by God.

In First Thessalonians 2:4, the apostle Paul described his experience with the fire of God at work in his life. He said, "But as we were allowed of God to be put in trust with the gospel, even so we speak; not as pleasing men, but God, which trieth our hearts." We've noted that the word "allowed" here is the Greek word *dokimadzo*, and it means *to test, to examine, to inspect,* or *to scrutinize.* Therefore, we could translate Paul's words as:

- "...We were *tested* of God..."
- "...We were *examined* of God..."
- "...We were *inspected* of God..."
- "...We were *scrutinized* of God..."

The word *dokimadzo* was used for a test to determine the quality or sincerity of a thing, and once the object being tested finally passed the test, it was viewed as genuine, sincere, and ready for use.

Moreover, the term *dokimadzo* was also employed to illustrate the test used to verify if coins were real or counterfeit. After a scrutinizing test by fire was performed on the coins, the coins that were real would stand up to the test, but the counterfeit ones would fail.

The word *dokimadzo* was also used to picture *the refining of metal*.

The Greek word *dokimadzo* was also used to describe the refining of metal by fire to remove its impurities. First, the metal was placed in a fire that burned at a certain degree of heat in order to bring the impurities in the metal to the surface so the refiner could remove them. Then for a second time, the metal was placed in another fire that burned even hotter. After the refiner scraped off the impurities, the metal was placed in the third and hottest fire with a temperature of 1,300 degrees. Thus, all three degrees of fire were needed to remove all the unseen impurities in the metal that were not visible to the naked eye. This is where we get the saying "*Stop putting me through the third degree.*"

Although this metal may have looked strong and ready for use even prior to these tests, it wasn't. There were unseen defects resident in the metal that would have shown up later as a break, fracture, or some kind of malfunction. Thus, before a person could be assured that the metal was free of defects and ready to be used, these three purifying tests at three varying degrees of blazing hot fire were required. The fire was hot, and the process was lengthy. But the tests were necessary in order to produce a good, reliable product.

Paul said the testing he experienced was overseen by God.

The word "of" here is the Greek word *hupo*, which means *by, directly by, under*, or *under the guidance of*. The inclusion of the word *hupo* tells us that God was the One who was orchestrating Paul's refinement. It was God who brought Paul through three different degrees of blazing fire over several years to expose and remove the impurities in his character that later would have shown up as a fracture or a malfunction that may have resulted in injury to others.

There are many people who are extremely gifted, but they began their ministry or career without embracing the fire of God. As a result, the character flaws and defects in their life surfaced as they became more well known, and their imperfections that were not dealt with ended up hurting both them and many who were following them.

Paul concluded First Thessalonians 2:4 by saying, "…Even so we speak; not as pleasing men, but God, which trieth our hearts." The word "trieth" here is again the Greek word *dokimadzo*, only in this verse the tense is continuous, which means the fiery tests never end. Although none of us like the preparation process, we need to learn to embrace it because God is always preparing us for future advancements.

Taking into account the original Greek meanings, here is the *Renner Interpretive Version (RIV)* of First Thessalonians 2:4:

> **It was a lengthy process, and I went through a lot of refining fires to get to this place, but I finally passed the test, and God saw that I was genuinely ready…and it's not over because God is still testing our hearts to see if we're ready for the next big step.**

'Saul' Needed Time To Become 'Paul'

When Paul — who was initially called Saul — met Jesus on the road to Damascus and surrendered his life to Him, he was immediately saved, anointed, and called to be an apostle (*see* Acts 9). However, he was not ready to be launched into ministry due to the rawness of his character. This is evident as we read toward the end of Acts 9, where the Bible says, "And when Saul was come to Jerusalem, he assayed to join himself to the disciples: but they were all afraid of him, and believed not that he was a disciple" (Acts 9:26).

Did you catch the serious flaw in Saul's character? The fact that he "assayed to join himself to the disciples" speaks of pride in his heart. It seems that because he held a prestigious position among the Jews before coming to Christ, he assumed he should instantly hold a high position among Christians once he was saved.

In addition to Saul's presumptuous attitude, his demeanor was raw and unbridled. In fact, he was so abrasive the Bible says the disciples were "…afraid of him, and believed not that he was a disciple" (Acts 9:26).

Surprisingly, despite these glaring defects in Saul's life, there was one man who believed in Paul, and that was Barnabas. The Bible says, "But Barnabas took him, and brought him to the apostles, and declared unto them how he had seen the Lord in the way, and that he had spoken to him, and how he had preached boldly at Damascus in the name of Jesus" (Acts 9:27).

When we come to Acts 9:29, we find something interesting about Saul's character. It says, "And he spake boldly in the name of the Lord Jesus, and disputed against the Grecians: but they went about to slay him." Now, on the surface, speaking boldly sounds good, but if we dig a little deeper, we find that Saul also "disputed against the Grecians," which in Greek means he argued against the Gentiles, so much so that they were about to kill him!

In Acts 9:30, it says, "…When the brethren knew [that Saul's life was in jeopardy], they brought him down to Caesarea, and sent him forth to Tarsus." This verse tells us that the apostles in Jerusalem were initially unaware of Saul's actions, which means Saul was acting on his own authority, not the authority God had established. The truth is, he didn't understand spiritual authority because he was a new believer. When the church leaders in Jerusalem heard of Saul's out-of-control behavior, they put him on a boat and sent him back to his hometown of Tarsus.

What was the result of the leadership's actions? We find it in Acts 9:31: "Then had the churches rest throughout all Judaea and Galilee and Samaria, and were edified; and walking in the fear of the Lord, and in the comfort of the Holy Ghost, were multiplied." When they got Saul out of town, peace and order were restored to the churches, and they were finally able to rest and breathe a sigh of relief.

Keep in mind, we are talking about the legendary apostle Paul who wrote nearly half the New Testament, planted churches, and spread the Gospel across most of the ancient world. As productive as he was during his missionary journeys, he did not start out that way. When he first came to Christ, his life was raw, unbridled, and riddled with character flaws. He needed to be refined by the fire of God so that he could fulfill the calling on his life. The same is true for you.

How Long Was Paul Absent From the Church Scene?

Although the Bible doesn't say how long Saul (Paul) was out of the picture, it does tell us how he reengaged with the Christian community. When the Spirit of God began moving powerfully among the Gentiles in Antioch, "Then departed Barnabas to Tarsus, for to seek Saul: And when he had found him, he brought him unto Antioch. And it came to pass, that a whole year they assembled themselves with the church, and taught much people…" (Acts 11:25,26).

Antioch was a "fiery" experience for Saul. God used this newly emerging church environment to expose and eliminate his character flaws and weaknesses before launching him into ministry. Acts 13:1 tells us about the leadership team at Antioch. It says, "Now there were in the church that was at Antioch certain prophets and teachers; as Barnabas, and Simeon that was called Niger, and Lucius of Cyrene, and Manaen, which had been brought up with Herod the tetrarch, and Saul."

Here is a quick review of the five co-leaders of the church in Antioch:

Barnabas was a distant Jew from the tribe of Levi who grew up in the Gentile country of Cyprus, which was a region in Greece (*see* Acts 4:36). Because he was raised so far from Jerusalem, it is likely that he didn't grow up around the strict religious environment that was so characteristic of that city.

Simeon was referred to as "Niger," which is the Latin word for *black*. Scholars speculate that this indicates Simeon was probably a black man from Africa and may have even been the slave of a Roman family at some point earlier in his life.

Lucius was from Cyrene, a region in Northern Africa. The name "Lucius" means *light* or *bright*. Like Simeon, it is likely that Lucius was also a black man and possibly a former slave.

Manaen had been brought up with Herod the tetrarch and was, in fact, likely a relative of Herod. Thus, he received a Roman education and grew up in a pagan society. This is significant because educated Romans were raised to look down on and even despise foreigners — especially Jews.

Saul — who became the apostle Paul — was the only theologically trained among all the co-leaders. Born into a very well-connected, tremendously wealthy Jewish family, Saul was afforded the best education money could buy. Before coming to Christ, he served as a rabbi and Pharisee, which means he was the most religiously instructed and possessed the greatest breadth of scriptural knowledge of any of his co-leaders in Antioch.

The Big Picture: Paul — the highly theologically trained Jewish scholar — was serving side by side with three Gentiles (Simeon, Lucius, and Manaen) and one Jew (Barnabas) who was not theologically trained. God used this unlikely assemblage of Jews and Gentiles and the environment of the new prototype church to mold and shape Paul into the one-of-a-kind apostle that would change history.

Paul Learned To Respect Those Who Were Different

At first glance, when you read Acts 13, it appears that Paul was quickly launched into full-time ministry, but if we dig a bit deeper into Early Church history, we find that he served as a co-leader at the church of Antioch for about eight years. During that time, he had to learn to respect Gentiles whom God was saving and adding to the Church. These were people who didn't have the same theological training and, in most cases, came from different economic and ethnic backgrounds than Paul.

Without question, learning to submit to individuals so vastly different than himself was a fiery test at times. There were probably moments when Paul must have said to himself, *Will I ever get out of here? Will the day ever come when I'm finally launched into my own ministry?* Like many Christians, Paul probably had his eye on the clock.

Do *you* have your eye on the clock? As we've noted previously, God is not a clock watcher — He is a character watcher. God was observing Saul's character as He allowed the heat to be turned up in his circumstances. As the fire burned, pride and prejudice were removed from Saul's life and replaced with humility and impartiality. Little by little, maturity was built into his character, making him spiritually strong and more Christlike.

The day finally came when God saw that Saul's character had been refined to the level it needed to be in order for him to begin his apostolic ministry. Acts 13:2 captures that moment. It says, "As they ministered to the Lord, and fasted, the Holy Ghost said, Separate me Barnabas and Saul for the work whereunto I have called them."

Clearly, this was an exciting moment for Saul. But is it possible that his launch into ministry could have come earlier had he embraced the holy fire that God was bringing to refine him? Yes, it's possible. The fact is, how long we stay in the fire depends on our response to it. If we resist, fight, or run from the fire of God, we will extend our time of waiting and delay the blessings God has planned.

Embrace the Fire!

Remember, the testing of our character is never ending. That is what the apostle Paul tells us in First Thessalonians 2:4. God desires to continue to advance us into new places and positions, but before He can open up a new opportunity, He has to place us in a new "oven" to burn off the excess and eliminate the defects and weaknesses in our lives.

Friend, the greater your assignment, the greater the period of preparation is required. Instead of resisting or running from the fire, ask God for His grace to embrace the place where He put you. God is an all-consuming fire, and as you draw near to Him, His presence will begin to burn out of you everything that could later affect you or others in a negative way.

STUDY QUESTIONS

> **Study to shew thyself approved unto God, a workman that needeth not to be ashamed, rightly dividing the word of truth.**
> **— 2 Timothy 2:15**

1. Acts 13:1 lists four men who served as co-leaders with the apostle Paul at the church of Antioch: Barnabas, Simeon, Lucius, and Manaen. What new insights did you learn about these leaders?

2. As challenging as relationships can be at times, we need people in our lives. Paul learned firsthand that believers who share the same faith — even those who are quite different than us — are vital to us experiencing spiritual maturity and fulfilling our God-ordained destiny. What do these scriptures speak to you personally about the importance of godly friends in your life?
   - Proverbs 17:17; 27:17

- Ecclesiastes 4:8-12
- Matthew 18:19,20
- Exodus 17:8-13 and Nehemiah 4:15,16

PRACTICAL APPLICATION

> But be ye doers of the word, and not hearers only,
> deceiving your own selves.
> —James 1:22

1. At the church in Antioch, God used an unlikely group of people from vastly different educational and ethnic backgrounds to mold and shape Paul into the person he needed to be to fulfill his calling. Who has God placed around you that is almost annoyingly different and seems incompatible to work with?

2. Get quiet before God and pray, *Lord, how are You working through this person/group to prepare me for what You have planned for me? What strengths are they designed to sharpen, or what weaknesses are they designed to expose? Please open my eyes to see what You're doing in my life so I can cooperate better with Your process. In Jesus' name. Amen.*

3. Despite the glaring defects of pride and prejudice in Saul's life, Barnabas — whose name means "son of encouragement" — saw the gift of God on Saul's life and took a personal interest in helping him grow in his faith. Who has been like a *Barnabas* in your life? Who has spoken up for you when others pushed you away? Who has made an intentional, sustained effort to help you grow in your faith? If possible, reach out today and express your appreciation and gratefulness to this person.

LESSON 5

TOPIC

Fire Is Required if You Want To Have Gold in Your Life

SCRIPTURES

1. **1 Thessalonians 2:4** — But as we were allowed of God to be put in trust with the gospel, even so we speak; not as pleasing men, but God, which trieth our hearts.
2. **Hebrews 12:29** — For our God is a consuming fire.

GREEK WORDS

1. "allowed" — δοκιμάζω (*dokimadzo*): to test; to examine; to inspect; to scrutinize; to determine the quality or sincerity of a thing; the object scrutinized has passed the test, so it can now be viewed as genuine and sincere; this word δοκιμάζω (*dokimadzo*) was used to illustrate the test used to determine real and counterfeit coinage; after a scrutinizing test was performed, the bona fide coinage would stand up to the test and the counterfeit would fail; this word δοκιμάζω (*dokimadzo*) was used to picture the refining of metal by fire to remove its impurities; first, the metal was placed in a fire that burned at a certain degree of heat; then, it was placed in a fire burning at an even higher degree; and finally, it was placed in a blazing fire that burned at the highest degree of all; three such tests were needed in order to remove from the metal all the unseen impurities that were hidden from the naked eye; from the viewpoint of the naked eye, the metal probably looked strong and ready to be used even prior to those tests, but unseen defects were resident in the metal that would have shown up later as a break, fracture, or some kind of malfunction; before a person could be assured that the metal was free of defects and thus ready to be used, these three purifying tests at three different degrees of blazing hot fire were required; the fire was hot and the process was lengthy, but the tests were necessary in order to achieve a good product

2. "of" God — ὑπὸ (*hupo*): by; directly by; under; under the guidance of

3. "trieth" — δοκιμάζω (*dokimadzo*): a form of the same word, but here in a continuous sense
4. "consuming" — καταναλίσκω (*katanalisko*): a compound of κατά (*kata*) and ἀναλίσκω (*analisko*); the preposition κατά (*kata*) here, is an intensifier and denotes a downward action, and the word ἀναλίσκω (*analisko*) means to annihilate, consume, destroy, or devour; compounded, καταναλίσκω (*katanalisko*) means to consume from top to bottom, to consume utterly, to devour completely or wholly

SYNOPSIS

The fabulous Russian Gzhel we've been talking about in our lessons not only has the classic blue and white colors, but it can also have extravagant inlays of gold. Because gold is so valuable and tedious to work with, it must be applied to the vessel by a highly skilled master craftsman.

After the porcelain piece has emerged from the second oven, it makes its way to a special room where the gold is attached. What's interesting is that when the gold is first applied, it is black in color and difficult to see. It is the third exposure to fire that brings the brilliance of the gold to light. Thus, if a vessel is going to include gold, it will have to go through three separate firings.

Similarly, if we are going to have "gold" in our character, we're going to have to embrace the fire of God in our lives repeatedly. First Peter 1:7 (*NLT*) says, "…Trials will show that your faith is genuine. It is being tested as fire tests and purifies gold — though your faith is far more precious than mere gold. So when your faith remains strong through many trials, it will bring you much praise and glory and honor on the day when Jesus Christ is revealed to the whole world."

If you feel as if you're going through the fire, don't panic. God is likely at work purifying your character to make you stronger and bring out His vibrant colors in your life. As you lean into the process, the benefits you experience as a result will be more than worth the heat you endured to get there — and your capacity to work with and enjoy God will be greater than you ever imagined!

The emphasis of this lesson:

With each level of promotion comes a new fire we are to embrace. God Himself is a consuming fire, so when you have His manifest presence

in your life, you also have His refining fire at work. His fire comes to refine you, burning up the impurities and defects in your life that stand between you and the fulfillment of your destiny.

A Final Review of Lessons 1 – 4

As we have seen in all our previous lessons, before Paul was entrusted with the Gospel and launched into his apostolic ministry, God brought him through a process of preparation. In First Thessalonians 2:4, Paul describes this process by saying, "But as we were allowed of God to be put in trust with the gospel, even so we speak; not as pleasing men, but God, which trieth our hearts."

The word "allowed" is the Greek word *dokimadzo*. It means *to test*, *to examine*, *to inspect*, or *to scrutinize*. Hence, Paul was saying, "We were tested, examined, inspected, and scrutinized by God." This word *dokimadzo* was used to determine the quality or sincerity of a thing, and once the object being scrutinized had passed the test, it was now seen as genuine and sincere.

The term *dokimadzo* was used to illustrate types of testing. First, it described the test that determined real and counterfeit coinage. After a scrutinizing test of fire was performed, the bona fide coinage would stand up to the test and the counterfeit would fail.

Most importantly, the word *dokimadzo* was used to picture the refining of metal by fire to remove its impurities. First, the metal was placed in a fire that burned at a certain degree of heat. Then it was placed in a second fire burning at an even higher degree. Finally, it was placed in a third blazing inferno that burned at the highest degree of all. Each time, the fire caused impurities in the metal to separate and rise to the surface. The refiner would then remove them, leaving behind a purer, stronger form of metal.

Three fiery tests were needed to remove all the unseen impurities from the metal that were hidden from the naked eye. Although the metal probably looked strong and ready to be used even prior to those tests, unseen defects were resident in the metal that would have shown up later as a break, fracture, or some type of malfunction. Therefore, before a person could be assured the metal was free of defects and thus ready to be used, three purifying tests at three different degrees of blazing hot fire were required. The fire was hot and the process was lengthy, but the tests were necessary in order to achieve a good, usable, and reliable material.

Paul used the word *dokimadzo* to describe the testing God had brought him through. By using this word, it was the equivalent of Paul saying, "God put me through three degrees of blazing hot fire. By putting me through the third degree, He removed unseen impurities in my character that were hidden from my eyes — defects and flaws I couldn't see that would have weakened my ministry and caused major problems down the road for me and others."

It was the different intensity levels of fire that effectively prepared Paul for apostolic ministry. We saw that his place of preparation was the church in Antioch, and Scripture says he served as a co-leader with four other men there for about eight years (*see* Acts 13:1). The mix of Gentiles and Jews and the diversity of their ethnicity, education, and background were all used by God to forge Paul into the pioneering apostle he was called to be.

Paul specifically said the testing he experienced was "of God." The word "of" here is the Greek word *hupo*, which means *by*, *directly by*, *under*, or *under the guidance of.* The use of this word tells us clearly that the fire Paul went through was not from the devil. It was a refinement applied *directly by God* and *under God's personal guidance*.

Paul went on to say, "...Even so we speak; not as pleasing men, but God, which trieth our hearts" (1 Thessalonians 2:4). The word "trieth" is again the Greek word *dokimadzo*, but here it is used in a continuous sense, which indicates not only did Paul and his ministry associates go through fire in the past, they were also being tested regularly by God to prepare them for future advancements.

When God saw that Paul's character had been refined to the level it needed to be in order for him to begin his apostolic ministry, the Holy Spirit launched him into ministry. The Bible says, "As they ministered to the Lord, and fasted, the Holy Ghost said, Separate me Barnabas and Saul for the work whereunto I have called them" (Acts 13:2).

Taking into account the original Greek meanings, here is the *Renner Interpretive Version (RIV)* of First Thessalonians 2:4:

> **It was a lengthy process, and I went through a lot of refining fires to get to this place, but I finally passed the test, and God**

saw that I was genuinely ready...and it's not over because God is still testing our hearts to see if we're ready for the next big step.

Again, the bigger the assignment, the longer the period of preparation.

With Each Promotion Comes a New Fire

It's important to note the fact that "...our God is a consuming fire" (Hebrews 12:29). This truth is foundational to the character of God and is also stated in Deuteronomy 4:24. Here, the word "consuming" is the Greek word *katanalisko*, which is a compound of *kata* and *analisko*. The preposition *kata* serves as an intensifier and denotes *a downward action*, and the word *analisko* means *to annihilate, consume, destroy*, or *devour*. When these words are compounded, the new word *katanalisko* means *to consume from top to bottom; to consume utterly; to devour completely or wholly*.

In light of this word *katanalisko* — the word translated here as "consuming" — we see that when you have God's presence in your life, you also have His fire. And the greater the manifestation of His presence, the greater the fire that is at work burning up impurities and defects. When the fire comes, it is there to refine us and make us better — not to hurt or destroy us.

As God's children, we are all meant to experience His fire. We've seen that Saul, who became the apostle Paul, repeatedly experienced the fire of God. Likewise, so did Abraham and Sarah, their son of promise Isaac, as well as Jacob, Joseph, Jonah, and Moses. Once more, Rick shared how he, too, experienced God's fire when he was first attending a university church. He said:

> When I was involved in a church at my university, I really believed my gifts outshined everyone else's. Consequently, I went to the leadership of the church and said, 'Hey, you need to understand who I am because I'm such a gift to you.'
>
> I was studying the Greek New Testament, and I was smart — and I knew it. I arrogantly thought that everyone needed me. So I told the church leaders to give me a place of ministry, and they gave me one. 'Rick, you are in charge of vacuuming all the carpets and setting up all the folding chairs.' Not too long after that, they reassigned me to washing dishes.

Needless to say, I was very offended. I just couldn't believe they would ask someone as gifted as me to vacuum, wash dishes, and set up the chairs. After all, I was God's gift to that church…or so I thought. But God had put me in the oven of preparation to get me ready for my future.

Initially, I grumbled, mumbled, and complained while vacuuming, setting up the chairs, and washing the dishes. *Why am I not in the pulpit teaching*, I thought. But in time, God began revealing to me that I wanted to *be served* rather than serve, and I wanted to shine before it was my time. Indeed, God really used that season to burn some defects out of my character. When I look back now, I can see how true Paul's words were in First Thessalonians 2:4. Here again is the *Renner Interpretive Version (RIV)* of it:

It was a lengthy process, and I went through a lot of refining fires to get to this place, but I finally passed the test, and God saw that I was genuinely ready…and it's not over because God is still testing our hearts to see if we're ready for the next big step.

Like Paul, Rick did pass the test, and he went on to teach the Word of God in that university with great passion. But that fiery test was just the beginning. After moving to another state, he joined the staff of a huge denominational church and began serving as an assistant to the senior pastor. Rick couldn't have been more thrilled to have that position. It seemed as though a massive door of opportunity had opened, and it had. But what Rick didn't understand is that he had also stepped into a new fire. He explains…

> That assistant pastor position was the most fiery experience I'd ever had in my life up until that moment. God Himself put me into that oven, placing me under a very strong spiritual leader who required things of me that no one had ever required.
>
> Initially, my gifts were shining, and my part of the church was growing. Although people were talking about how the whole church was growing, the truth is the whole church was growing because *my* part of the church was growing, and I was so proud of myself.

Well, my pastor saw the pride in my life, and God used him to address it in a rather unusual way. I can still remember how he would say, 'Rick, you're doing such a great job, but my car really needs to be washed.' He would then hand me his keys and say, 'Please go wash my car, and when you're finished, go ahead and vacuum the interior and buff the outside so it shines.'

I remember thinking, *Oh great. Here we go again with the carpet.*

Then he would say, 'While you're out, I want you to take a couple pairs of my shoes over to the shoe shop and have them shined.' Reluctantly, I did everything he asked. I washed, vacuumed, and buffed out the car — and got his shoes shined, of course.

No sooner had his brief 'thank you' left his lips, he would start back in and say, 'You know, Rick, there's a lot of leaves in my yard that need to be raked, and I don't have time to do it. Would you please do me a favor and go over to my house and rake all the leaves?'

I remember looking at him thinking, *What in the world are you talking about? Are you kidding me? God sent me to be a blessing to you, and you're asking me to use my anointing to rake leaves.* Even so, as frustrated as I was, I'd go to his house, get out the rake, and begin raking. His yard was simply enormous. It seemed like there were trees as far as the eye could see. I just kept raking and raking and raking. The job felt like it was never-ending because once I raked the leaves, I also had to bag the leaves. These kinds of tasks went on day after day, week after week, and month after month.

Meanwhile, along with seeing the pride in my life, my pastor also saw my lack of discipline. To address this issue, he required me to meet him every morning at 5:30. Now, my wife, Denise, and I had just gotten married, and I wanted to be home with her — not having coffee with the pastor at 5:30 in the morning. But he was the boss.

I can still see him sitting in his usual spot, staring at his watch as I walked in. And if I arrived to the meeting one minute late, as soon as I got to the table, he'd say, 'Now tell me why you couldn't be here on time?'

His dealings with me about being disciplined also spilled over into the area of my finances. In fact, he assigned someone to help me learn how to manage my money more efficiently. It came to the point where it seemed like that pastor had his fingers in every single part of my life. Can you say, 'Blazing fire'? That's what I was in…but it was a fire I desperately needed.

That fiery furnace revealed that I had an issue of pride and arrogance as well as a lack of discipline in several areas of my life, including how to handle my time and my finances. It also showed me that I really didn't understand submission to authority, which I really needed to learn so that I could grow into the leader God needed me to be.

Looking back, I can see that God loved me so much He put me into that blazing hot oven of ministry and kept me there in order to reveal my flaws and burn them out of my life. And like a 'consuming fire' (*katanalisko*), He burned them out from the top all the way to the bottom — He utterly consumed my impurities, completely and wholly devouring them so that I would be ready to launch forward into the ministry to which God called me.

What's interesting is that Rick said when he thinks of those fiery years at the university church and his time serving as an assistant to that strong-willed pastor, they continue to be some of the most wonderful moments of his life. Although he didn't enjoy the fire at that time, he realizes that if he hadn't gone through those experiences and embraced them, he would have carried all kinds of impurities with him even to this day — defects that would have shown up as flaws or a malfunction later in life, and negatively affected him, his family, and many others.

Friend, God loves you, and His purpose for bringing fire into your life is to lovingly eliminate the very things that stand between you and the fulfillment of your destiny. He is not trying to hurt you but to *help* you by making you stronger, cutting off the unneeded excess, and bringing out the God-colors in your life. Jesus said, "…You're here to be light, bringing out the God-colors in the world. God is not a secret to be kept. We're going public with this, as public as a city on a hill" (Matthew 5:14 *MSG*).

As you complete this study, take time to pray: *Lord, You are a consuming fire, so as I draw near to You, I'm asking that Your fire would burn up all the impurities and defects out of my life. Help me to embrace and not resist Your fire*

The Fire of God in Your Life | 45

so that I am strong and thoroughly prepared for what You have called me to do. In Jesus' name. Amen!

STUDY QUESTIONS

> **Study to shew thyself approved unto God, a workman that needeth not to be ashamed, rightly dividing the word of truth.**
> — 2 Timothy 2:15

1. As refining fire tests and tries, it also consumes everything that is combustible or flammable, and its presence and power are undeniable. What did God's fire do and prove in Genesis 15:8-21 (Note key verses: 17 and 18); Exodus 13:21,22; First Kings 18:36-39? How did His fiery presence affect everyone present?

2. Just like God showed up as a consuming fire in the lives of Abraham, Moses, and Elijah, when you give Him a sacrifice of praise, His presence shows up in a powerful way. What does Scripture say He'll do for you as you come close to Him in worship and brokenness? (*See* James 4:8; Psalm 22:3; 34:17-19; 51:16,17; Isaiah 66:2)?

3. What might our life be like if we *reject* and *run from* God's fire? Jonah's life is a sobering example and offers valuable insight into our own plight.

    - What did God tell Jonah to do? What did Jonah actually do? (*See* Jonah 1:1-3.)

    - How did God respond to Jonah's disobedience of going to Tarshish? (*See* Jonah 1:4-17.)

    - What action did Jonah take when God brought this fire into his life? (*See* Jonah 2:1-10.)

    - What was Jonah's attitude *after* the people of Nineveh genuinely repented and received God's forgiveness? What impurities do you notice in his attitude? (*See* Jonah 4:1-11.)

    - What do you think God was trying to tell Jonah in Jonah 4:6-11? What is He showing *you*?

    - Who do you find it hard to reach out to or be happy for? Ask God to show you why and allow Him to remove the impurities that surface.

PRACTICAL APPLICATION

> But be ye doers of the word, and not hearers only,
> deceiving your own selves.
> —James 1:22

1. Remember the second fire Rick described? The pastor he worked for expected more of him than he ever planned to give, but years later, Rick could see how that season was really a *gift* to help him succeed as a leader. Who has been a leader in your life that expected a lot from you? What did they require that seemed so hard for you to deliver? What can you now see that you gained or learned from that fiery experience?

2. When we find ourselves in a new, God-arranged fire, it often feels very uncomfortable and unnatural. So, it takes us awhile to embrace the work He's trying to do. What is a fire you're in the middle of right now that's been very hard to embrace? Which areas of your life is it refining? Ask God to help you see the purpose of why He's brought you here and the grace you need to cooperate so that the process isn't delayed. Make sure you journal whatever He shows you.

Notes

Notes

CLAIM YOUR FREE RESOURCE!

As a way of introducing you further to the teaching ministry of Rick Renner, we would like to send you FREE of charge his teaching, "How To Receive a Miraculous Touch From God" on CD or USB format.

In His earthly ministry, Jesus commonly healed *all* who were sick of *all* their diseases. In this profound message, learn about the manifold dimensions of Christ's wisdom, goodness, power, and love toward all humanity who came to Him in faith with their needs.

☑ YES, I want to receive Rick Renner's monthly teaching letter!

Simply scan the QR code to claim this resource or go to: renner.org/claim-your-free-offer

WITH US!

renner.org

facebook.com/rickrenner • facebook.com/rennerdenise

youtube.com/rennerministries • youtube.com/deniserenner

instagram.com/rickrrenner • instagram.com/rennerministries_
instagram.com/rennerdenise

www.ingramcontent.com/pod-product-compliance
Lightning Source LLC
Chambersburg PA
CBHW061302040426
42444CB00010B/2474